Contents

Why do we eat?

We eat food to help us live and grow. Food gives us **energy** for running and playing. We enjoy the taste of our food.

level

2

What We Eat

Brenda Stones

KINGFISHER

KINGFISHER

First published 2013 by Kingfisher
an imprint of Macmillan Children's Books
a division of Macmillan Publishers Limited
20 New Wharf Road, London N1 9RR
Basingstoke and Oxford
Associated companies throughout the world
www.panmacmillan.com

Series editor: Heather Morris
Literacy consultant: Hilary Horton

ISBN: 978-0-7534-3090-3
Copyright © Macmillan Publishers Ltd 2013

9 8 7 6 5 4 3 2 1

1TR/1012/WKT/UG/105MA

A CIP catalogue record for this book is available from the British Library.

Printed in China

Picture credits
The Publisher would like to thank the following for permission to reproduce their material.
Every care has been taken to trace copyright holders. However, if there have been unintentional
omissions or failure to trace copyright holders, we apologize and will, if informed, endeavour
to make corrections in any future edition.

Top = t; Bottom = b; Centre = c; Left = l; Right = r Cover Shutterstock/Monkey Business Images;
Pages 3t Shutterstock/Monkey Business Images; 3ct Photolibrary/Fresh Food Images; 3c Shutterstock/MikeE
3cb Photolibrary/Corbis; 3b Photolibrary/81a Productions; 4 Photolibrary/Aflo Foto Agency; 5t Photolibrary/
Julia Martin; 5b Photolibrary/Stockbroker; 6 Shutterstock/Larisa Lofitskaya; 7t Nutshell Media/Masanori
Kobayashi; 7b Nutshell Media/David Cumming; 8 Shutterstock/Monkey Business Images; 9 Kingfisher
Artbank; 10 Shutterstock/ MikeE; 11t Shutterstock/Bratwustle; 11b Shutterstock/Nagy-Bagoly Arpad;
12t Shutterstock/ Tish1; 12b Shutterstock/Shmel; 13t Shutterstock/MikeE; 13b Photolibrary/ Fresh Food
Images; 14 Photolibrary/OJO Images; 15t Shutterstock/Cristi Lucaci; 15b Photolibrary/ Fresh Food Images;
16 Photolibrary/Cusp; 17t Shutterstock/Glenda M. Powers; 17b Photolibrary/Corbis; 18–19 Corbis/moodboard
19t Corbis/Paul Thompson; 20 Shutterstock/Krivosheev V; 21t Corbis/image 100; 21b Photolibrary/Blend
Images; 22 Corbis/Ocean; 23t Shutterstock/Benis Arapovic; 23b Shutterstock/Losevsky Pavel;
24 Shutterstock/paul Prescott; 25t Shutterstock/Terence Mendoza; 25b Shutterstock/Monkey Business
Images; 26 Photolibrary/MIXA; 27t Corbis/Food Passionated; 27b Shutterstock/mtr; 28 Shutterstock/
swissmacky; 29 Photolibrary/ Fresh Food Images; 30 Photolibrary/Image Source; 31t Photolibrary/81a
Productions; 31b Photolibrary/Lineair; 32l Shutterstock/Larisa Lofitskaya; 32c Shutterstock/Cristi Lucaci;
32r Shutterstock/Krivosheev Vitaly.

It is fun to sit and eat our meals together, at home, at school or at a party.

When do we eat?

Most people have several meals each day. The first meal is **breakfast**.

Some people have a big meal in the middle of the day. Others eat later in the evening.

People have different names for their meals, like lunch, dinner and tea. What do you call your meals?

What do we eat?

We need to eat a good mix of food to stay **healthy**.

Try to eat a mix of all the foods on his plate every day.

some meat, fish, eggs or beans

bread, potatoes, rice or pasta

some milk or cheese

not too much cake, chocolate or fried foods

lots of fruit and vegetables

Fruit and vegetables

Fruit and vegetables all come from plants. They help to keep you healthy.

There are lots of different sorts of fruit and vegetables. They grow in different parts of the world.

We can cook vegetables in different ways. Many vegetables can be eaten **raw**.

Which is your favourite fruit or vegetable?

Bread, rice and pasta

Bread, rice and pasta
all give you energy.
They come from
grains, like wheat
and rye.

People all over the world eat bread. It can look very different and it can taste different, too.

Meat, fish and eggs

Meat, fish and eggs all help you grow. Fish oil is good for your heart and your brain.

You can cook meat, fish and eggs in lots of different ways to make them tasty.

Nuts, beans and lentils help you grow too. If you don't eat meat, fish and eggs, you need to eat these foods instead.

Milk, cheese and yoghurt

We call milk, cheese and yoghurt **dairy** foods. They help build our bones. Milk comes from cows, goats or sheep.

Milk can be made into other foods, like yoghurt and cheese. We often cook with cheese, and put it on pizza and pasta.

Ice cream is made from milk, too.

17

What to drink?

Your body needs lots of water to keep it working well. You need to drink about six glasses of water every day.

Drinking milk is good for your teeth and bones. Fizzy drinks are not good for you because they have lots of sugar in them.

A little fruit juice can be good for you too. This man is making oranges into juice.

Where does our food come from?

Most of our food comes from farms. Farmers grow grains, fruit and vegetables. They keep animals for milk and meat.

Fish comes from the sea and rivers.

Cutting a field of grain on a farm

Lots of food travels
across the world
in planes or boats.
But some people
grow their own
food at home.

What happens next?

Some food goes straight to a **factory** from the farm. Factories make grain into flour. Then they make the flour into bread, cakes or pasta.

Lots of food is put into tins, packets or boxes, to keep it fresh. The labels on the outside tell us what the food is made of.

Shopping

We buy our food from shops and markets. There are small shops, big **supermarkets** and street markets. Street markets sell mainly fresh food.

Small shops like **bakeries** and **fishmongers** sell one sort of food.

Supermarkets sell everything.

Cooking

We cook food to make it taste good.
There are lots of ways to cook food.

We can boil it in water. We can
grill it under or over heat.

We can fry it
n fat. We can
oast it in the
ven.

People in different countries cook
food in different ways. In Italy, they
cook pizza in an oven like this one.

Foods of the world

We often eat food that grows easily in our country.

In India, rice grows well in the hot, wet weather. In Africa, people eat a lot of yams, which are a bit like potatoes.

The foods in our supermarkets come from all around the world.

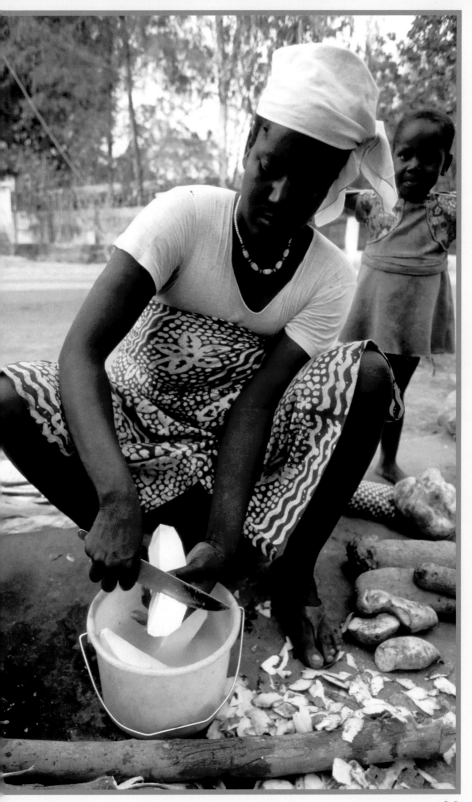

Food for feasts

Food is an important part of any feast or party. On your birthday, you may have a big cake.

or **Diwali**, people ake sweets. In ne USA, people ook pumpkin for **Thanksgiving**. At wedding, there ill be a feast.

haring food and eating together nakes us feel good!

Glossary

bakeries shops that sell bread

breakfast the first meal of the day

dairy milk, and foods made from milk

Diwali an important Hindu and Sikh festival when people light lamps and share sweets

energy the power that drives our bodies

factory a place where things are made

fishmongers shops that sell fish

grains the seeds of some plants, such as corn and wheat, that are ground to make flour

healthy fit and well

raw not cooked

supermarkets large shops that sell everything

Thanksgiving a holiday when people in the USA and Canada give thanks to God, friends and family